Journeying

Paul Sutherland was born in Ontario, Canada, in 1947, and arrived in the UK in 1973. He is founder and editor of the international literary journal *Dream Catcher*, and his own writing has appeared in more than fifty anthologies, newspapers and journals.

Previous collections of Paul's poetry include *Seven Earth Odes* (Endpapers Press, 2004) and *Spires and Minarets* (Sunk Island, 2010). He has an MA in English Literature from the University of York, and became both a Sufi Muslim and a freelance writer in 2004. He lives with his wife in Lincolnshire.

Also by Paul Sutherland

Spires and Minarets
April Renga
Selected Ben Nicholson Miniatures (with Mick Paine)
Holy Week Sequence
Seven Earth Odes
Mid Atlantic (CD, with Graeme Scott)
The Town Boy
Winter Poems

Journeying

PAUL SUTHERLAND

VALLEY

First published 2012 by Valley Press
Woodend, The Crescent, Scarborough, YO11 2PW
www.valleypressuk.com

ISBN: 978 1 908853 05 9
Cat. no. VP0036

Copyright © Paul Sutherland 2012

The right of Paul Sutherland to be identified as the
author of this work has been asserted in accordance with
the Copyright, Designs and Patents Act 1988

All rights reserved. No part of this publication may be
reproduced, stored in or introduced into a retrieval system,
or transmitted in any form, by any means (electronic,
mechanical, photocopying, recording or otherwise) without
prior written permission from the rights holders.

9 8 7 6 5 4 3 2 1

A CIP record for this book is
available from the British Library

Printed and bound in Great Britain by
Imprint Digital, Upton Pyne, Exeter

This book is sold subject to the condition that it shall not,
by way of trade or otherwise, be lent, resold, hired out,
or otherwise circulated without the publisher's prior
consent in any form of binding or cover other than that
in which it is published and without a similar condition,
including this condition, being imposed on the
subsequent purchaser.

Front cover photograph: RedWolf
Back cover photograph: Janice Jackson

www.valleypressuk.com/authors/paulsutherland

To my Grandparents
Ernest and Violet Rycroft
and my Dad and Mum
John and Lorraine Sutherland

Earth, this dust-fine oldness and love
always whole, always wandering, like glass.

Acknowledgements

Poems from *Journeying* have appeared in: *Nassau Review* (USA), *Contemporary Literary Horizon, Pendulum* (Avalanche Books), *Mid Atlantic* (Poetry Book Society/ Apples and Snakes), *North Yorkshire One Nine Nine* (Sutton Press), *The Exhibitionists* (Stairwell Books), *International Other Voices, Pennine Platform, Orbis, Airelings, Lincolnshire Echo, Dream Catcher, Brando's Hat, Nightingale, PTO, The Thinker, Text Bones, The Threshing Floor, Poetry New Zealand* (NZ), *Fin, Tadeeb International,* and *English* (Oxford Journals).

'Diver' was selected as a poem to be used in promoting the London 2012 Olympics.

Contents

I.

The Diver 11
My Foreign Land 12
After the Sadie Hawkins Dance 14
Grandpa's Day 16
Grandma's Night 17
1969 21
By Stoney Creek Battlefield 22
Another Last Morning in Canada 27
Sleaford View 30
Ash Moon Duo 31
Journeying 33

II.

Summer at No. 8 45
Harbour Mouth: Whitby 47
Infant Land 50
Up From the Coastal Route 51
Shadow of Earth 53
Two Gardeners 57
Somersby 58
The Deserter 59
The Waiting Room 61
At Asycoughfee 63
Canada – America 64
Last Words 70
At Staithes 72

III.

No Grimms, Andersen or Beatrix Potter 77
Hide and Seek 79
The Pond 80
She Wore Grey 81
I first saw this view 82
Red Hawthorn-Hedged 83

I.

The Diver

Perpendicular to the sheer cliff:
her caressing fingers ease around
pale ears, coax across the nape;
she guides and tucks her curls
until each haphazard glimmer's
hidden beneath her bathing cap.
Streamlined, she flexes, raising
her heels and bracing spread toes,
springs from the bony platform –
four billion stars in a diver's arc
– almost a soundless entry –
stroke for stroke sets out to sea.

My Foreign Land

On flight from Europe
I stare from my oblong porthole
at a winter panorama,
white and black template
tooled with eccentric figures –
lakes and rivers that curl
back through dark-greyness,
flowing below the ice
to the Gulf of St. Lawrence.

I long to descend into vastness
touch down on wind-scribbled snow
to see what survives on the edge of survival.
To pitch into the void
but feel snow and frost
forming cuffs on a leeward sapling,
small gradations to where a drift
dwindles to let the freckled rock
shine through, set tundra ablaze.

Once more I return – not to the land
I lived and dreamed through –
celebrating its silencing winter –
but my foreign land
from across the ocean.

Beside me a young English passenger.
Through the flight we've talked.
She's en route to her husband
in Canada. I call her to look,
she puts down her paperback,
leaning across then peers out,
her face gradually hardening
she exclaims *O it's so barren!*

I think of intimacy down there,
continuous freezing and releasing;
on finger-pads snow crystals melt
a star-tissue design inside each.
I think, perhaps, you can endure
close focus, detect with cultivated ears
the feather-paths of phantom walkers
inclining to instinct, who, with their
airy snow-shoes' footfall, followed
bowed shorelines of crumpling ice
along named waterways: first residents,
darker skinned than her or me, who
heard spring's thunderous trickle.

I ruminate on her last word *barren*,
glance through the roaring glass
then back and say under-breath:
'Canada barren? Never call it that.'

After the Sadie Hawkins Dance

Sunlight teases my listening eyes.
Jukebox music dances,
a car's window must be ajar.
Through air, new promises usher.

I listen to a younger self
promising after the Sadie Hawkins dance
to share with the beautiful and desired
a serpentine walk home –
between farewells and porch-lamps –
with no walls along sidewalk edges
to hold two interlopers
straying into the text of love.

I see now what you meant.
There was an open manuscript between us,
not the blank leaves of one I might dictate
but an extensive volume whose pages
were always flicking back and forth.
I know, by the look in your locked sight
that you wish you could've stopped the pages
and seen what had been written for us.

Far from disco song, I offer a lost landscape
with its sheltered navel and wind-torn head.
From my homeland, I give you a myth –
how the hero Nanabozho, shunned at birth,
switched himself to a rabbit and ate cool
moist grass as if seizing a moment of love.

Nanabozho (my little white rabbit) is a prototype trickster of the Ojbway tribe or language group in Canada; there are variations on his name across a wide range of First Nations.

Grandpa's Day

Quiet-footed, suicide often creeps up on its victim.
To understand cause (Albert Camus once probed)
you need to sniff out more than the grand seizure.
Sliver of regret, hair-line mischance, a so brief half-
heard damning, least detectable nudge towards hope,
anything can unhinge and trip someone into oblivion.

Quietly grandpa tripped into that same non-existence.
Not *taking* his life, but just past his eightieth birthday
with family engrossed round the leaf-lengthened table
he slipped out between the steaming roast and ice cream.
Among clacking of gathered china and noisy kitchen-talk,
without a warning gasp, slumped in his padded chair.
Nearby, a grandson's *are you ok, Papa?* left in space.

Grandma's Night

On a little stand
midpoint between her and me
lilies trumpeted a perfume
that subsumed love and ritual.
Except for her, resistant, yet sleeping.
Guessed she was sleeping.

I panned her living-room –
marble mantelpiece, glass-domed clock
mahogany stereo and a long oval table –
to her, superficially serene. No distance
between the fancy dining table's legs
and bedstead. Life had turned inward
so far. From her window,
like an anchoress's squint, she
forecast the destinies of passers-by.

Grandma wasn't snoring.
I wished she would. Then I'd know
she wasn't reading my thoughts.
This watching she would think
strange, unnecessary, a violation.
I hoped my observance a secret.
Let her sleep, she's ill. Needs
a full slumber, end of time repose.

I shared my night
with the lilies.
Their mythic petals
outlast our variations;
they're still in bloom
equidistant between her and me
at the core of something that never closes.

I breathed in their uncompromising scent
and again swelled with enough affection
to draw near, looking over at twisted white hair,
her violently creased face, pale riot of wrinkles,
until I sank back to my safe vantage.

Once, seeing my consternation,
she'd explained, when she began to hum
a tune, she could never sleep
against the memory inspired.
I'm still troubled hearing someone hum
at a train station or on a bus,
an unarticulated grief's spoken.
Why couldn't she speak with me?
Sequestered in sound's absence
now and then irrupted with gurgling breath
as if she choked on sleep.

When did we share
that worked-over loose thought?
When were we hand-fast allies?
I waited alone in the massive hot clothes store
as she rattled plastic hangers
along a shiny rod, clashing them back and forth,
hunting a dress, wanting an absent world to hear:
the colour, the imploring design.
I awaited the favoured:
bluish, cerise, 'in the pink', flowery, crazy-patterned or plain.
I don't know which one she kept or how many times curtains
were whipped across a changing cubicle before she decided.

She was furthest
from that frantic hunt for style and size,
clamminess of discovery,
the night she died, similar to this, at the cool nadir.
She, out of touch with self,
could renounce, as if
a body fiercely gripped
had been released.

My vigil:
in the end I felt guilty.
Afraid I'd ripped the lace sack
that encompasses love's source,
the heart pumping in a heart.
A true lover might deflect his gaze
sensing he's on the threshold of that inner-place
to listen so intently.

I calmed my conscience
that tried to hound me back
to my bed in the large kitchen
behind the wall from her stiff breathing
where earlier I'd first heard
an arrhythmic hum
that broke my doze,
compelling me to get up, come into her space
to begin this surveillance.

On her final midnight, toward dawn,
cut-off, I knew I'd be distant,
remotest from comforting her heart –
that knowledge rooted me hard to my place
and caused me to scan the dark living room
for a reply from life at its outermost point
to set against death at its nearest.

1969

Two youths, strangers on a campsite,
one Canadian, the other American,
shoot an NFL football back & forth
among shoreline pines of Michigan.
Brown polished spirals shattering
passive green. Ducking, faking, we
run patterns pro-style, knife-precise,
catching one toss at the boot straps,
even full stretch a juggling one-hander,
until every limb aching we crash down
on a spare picnic table's bench to chat.
'What' y' doin' after summer?' I ask.
— *I'm going to Vietnam. And you?*

By Stoney Creek Battlefield

Redhill Creek skipped
from the escarpment's
limestone rim
spring-ragged

to Stoney Creek
Battleground: in 1812
American invasion
struck its northern limit here.

You and I tried to avoid
violets. Lavender blues
and whites where contorted roots
shaped descending stairs.

As we stepped,
trout lilies' waxy leaves
created pools
in mostly leafless wood.

Let's sit down there.
Your finger pointed
to the creek's rocky fringe.

Settled. I asked,
'How would you describe
this sound?'

I hear layers, you replied,
a chatter, a meditation,
frequent deep gulps.
Like silver sounds.
Do you understand?
Upstream the way it flows
you can almost see its path.

'Molten, like lava', I returned,
my eyes dazzled
by its surface.

But tried to imagine
the lyrical ore
you were able to hear.

'What I'm interested in', almost shouting,
'is the green patches
around boulders,
how they cushion burble.'

A boyish instinct arose,
I claimed I could cross
without getting a soaker;
you winced, disbelieving.

Downstream, across a pool,
I watched a black dog's head, V-shaped
above the shimmer, leaving a wake,
and envisaged Manitou's muskrat
struggling back with its first clutch of earth.

Enthralled
by trickle, murmur, babble,
we hardly noticed
how we'd fused
on glacial debris.

Polished coppery foliage
overhead.
I guess it's time to leave.

In our absence
coltsfoot rings
and nodes on branch-tips
had grown to new intensity.

'How quickly,' I nudged,
'the sound changes' –
stretching out
our commentary –
'as soon as we leave the edge.'

'Can you believe it?
They're wanting
to build an expressway
up through here.
Any green, pave it?'

You suffered
my harsh words. *I didn't know
but the debate's been going on
elsewhere for years.*

Around thoughts
your image still played
with patience.

I tried to dream up
a syllabic miniature:

soft, bold, silver notes,
by flashes of trillium
Redhill Creek winding.

Taking off your shoe, shaking out
a trapped pebble,
you showed me your heel
worn vermilion-raw, skin split.

Out from under the trees
pathway broadening,
Let's walk on the grass, you said.

I started to narrate
that Laura Secord saved Canada:
hero of 1812.
'She ran and warned
the Yanks were on the march north.
She sits in cameo
on every box of best
Canadian chocolate,
a milk-maid.'

A young lawn cooling hurt feet
you held my thread.
Yes,
like the Saxon girl
who guided monks to Durham,
a safe place for Cuthbert's body to rest.
A cow-maid too,
you noted in passing.

Another Last Morning in Canada

Not far enough from night to awake,
at a screen window I listen to warm spring:
to red-wing blackbirds, mourning dove and cardinals.
In a hush, you scoot past
in my pyjama top.

At breakfast, apricot daffodils
angle from a child-mouthed vase
of hand-blown olive glass.
In its clear depths
droplet-speckled stems
dilate and disappear
toward discrete continents.

This, an ordinary return
but you who arrived with me
now make ready to depart
with lake fossils and other souvenirs.

Our jet's long wings fidget.
Ready for take-off, a flight attendant,
motto wing on her lapel, snaps shut
each left open storage compartment.
Our carry-on luggage with shoreline debris
side by side overhead.

Our plane skims vaporous forms –
a streamline pebble skips
cutting tips of grey waves.
Clouds and sun flicker.

Somewhere over the surface of Labrador
dying rays show cotton candy cumuli,
cratered pink and rouge mountains.

Up here our obstinate love's free of duty.
You've smuggled on board a ripe banana.
When whiffs start to wind through the dim cabin
I pretend to shield you from approaching scandal.

Absently gazing
you munch and say:
Perhaps we'll over-shoot,
come down in Sicily,
fill the rest of our lives with exotic pleasure.
The night ocean passes. You're asleep
as a new continent comes in range,
light tracing cornice of hazy cliffs.
I wish the pilot now would speak,
pin-point where we are, call out
each estuary and moor-crown's nickname.
But the fields' eccentric quilting
tells all I need to know.

Refusing to fall in love
with re-discovered land, our rigid bird keeps
altitude till the captain tickles it down
through the drowsiness of space
to awake in astounded-thrust
on ground's long runway. It coasts to a halt,
without folding wings round a shimmering body
looks at once to fall asleep.

As forecast, when worries about customs
confiscating our beach-collected stones
are forgotten, we meet your son
followed by a fast car journey;
once or twice we manage
to flick each other's fingernails,
playing out an urgency:
you bursting with conversation
in front passenger seat,
me cowering in the back.

As we draw near our separate interiors,
I remember morning's vase of daffodils
and consider how a flower's stem
severed half-way up the middle
can be eased apart.

Sleaford View

Above a Dutch styled roof-scape
the sun drops into lead guttering gloom
as a half-vanished ball of rose and
ochre. A lookout – as if an ornament
that Sleafordians once placed high
to honour an abstaining benefactor –
a pigeon coos from a stone gable's curl.
Across in Moneys' Yard – a big black
thumb, a sail-less windmill takes the view.

At the same time, somewhere else,
it snows with no imaginable end.
Lookouts shelter. It thickens roof tiles
into sweeps. Wind swirls. It fumes
until strongest street lights look askance,
out of touch from beams of creeping cars.
From eaves long icicles harden into trails
like candle wax; under a white mask
frozen waterways disappear. Here

the open River Slea ambles
under pedestrian bridges. By its bank
a swan's migratory wings remain furled
and through January stratus the light fails
without releasing a galaxy of whorled crystals.

Ash Moon Duo

Outside the cramped theatre,
after another gig on our tour,
I observed ash-white cloud
opening from a full moon.

That night
you didn't need your high beams.

We were silent, passing
the ruined tower of a land lighthouse
sprinkled with aluminium dust.

By the time we reached our hotel
vapours zoomed overhead,
visible when trapped
in grey-blue rays. You thought
they must be flights of smoke,
searched the horizon for a fire.

From our window
a big garden bled into night.
A topiary screened
gushing fountains
and from a gazebo
along walkways blurred figures
shouldered urns of stone.

I thought of my mother's ashes,
in which heartland to sprinkle them:
by Erewash where she'd learnt to swim,
over traces of a razed dancing-floor,
among cups in Spalding tulip fields?

About moon-set, the weather snapped.
The east threatened with violet pink.
Catching the night's tail-end
I curled up in our room's armchair
and dozed, until your wind-playing fingers
soothed my shoulders, announced a new day.

Journeying

In that long tradition
I once abandoned my father and mother, left them
bewildered at their beloved land's failure
to hold their child.
Bereaved, in the frailty of their age,
I've denied them a son's support
and comforting. Over there
nieces, cousins and nephews have matured
in my absence, almost untouchable.

Now I'm travelling at the end of one millennium
before the new beginning
in a single carriage train, a big rigid caterpillar
that's relinquished pads for shrilling wheels;
carried past heath, marsh and on the east
finger-shadowed fens, by fortresses of straw
past quickset boundaries and bronze trees
views of partial concern. Journeying

without feeling inland –
no breadth of a continent
as experienced in youth –
each mood of terrain inclines
gradually, rapidly, towards an unseen brink.

I give up on perspectives, as you did
(my blind brother) when darkness fell
across the afternoon of your years.

I'm moving along the edge of somewhere
that Romans conceived, toward margins of the sea.
I don't hear surf, only knowledge of its roar
in a proud district of an indifferent county
among an island people, who, I've been told,
once controlled a quarter of the globe
on which the sun failed to set.

From one peep of day to the next,
youths hurl stones and confront bullets
near the golden dome in Jerusalem.
Hope of peace turns vaporous; fair words
fade, new violence erupts, injustice continues
closer to home than that centre-of-the-world.
My ex-soldier friend: *do you know,
I couldn't believe it; when I arrived in Palestine in '47
how they hated us; those I'd come to protect.
Both sides hated us Brits. Hated my guts.*

Out the window, above village rooflines,
tarred shells of abandoned windmills,
tops severed, sometimes onion-shaped, look Islamic.
Ancaster knobbed finials of vulnerable steeples
in profile cut ladders to climb: things you no longer see
but visualise. As thoughts bend towards you,
sun's brightness foreshadows triumphal blue,
yet so rapidly cloud and rain darken
and sense falters.

I'm among centuries of communities,
market towns sown like seeds,
purling tributaries of the Witham
and spilt mahogany chestnuts.
At peace amidst town and field dwellers
who match the step of Roman standard-bearers,
who heard the Lancaster's tyres screech,
who know, below their station's viny ironwork,
bones of Anglo-Saxons rest, not far
from where the pea-sorting girls
with deft callused finger ends
worked on till day was done.

You've been denied perspective.
Here, the horizon isn't drawn
by land rising toward the sky,
it fades a geodesic curve
from one stand of trees
to the next, each more hazy,
dissipating as a series of heroic acts.

Blind to the future,
the press of time's concatenation
coupled in train of every second's events.
More than once
I've longed to abort the journey,
inset a shaft of blankness.

I'm a foreigner, constantly coming in.
Yearn to be free
from counter pulls of home against home.
Here, the Empire seeks to repair
the wasted hope of global importance;
but my first home searches beneath reddened sod,
trowels through settlements, vanished relics,
legends, stone-scalloped arrowheads of flint.

We're homelandless: First Nation, Palestinian, Colonist, Jew.
Stand in the same middle ground,
locked-in through lamp-strained chamber sessions
where forgiveness can't reclaim lost history.

Have you heard squadrons of metal swans' wings
with racket of cymbals battering the sky
as they lift from sedate meadows?
Heard hollowness of those returning –
mission done? Could you disentangle
nature, love, history? Pry them apart,
your heart drumming with longing
for the one thing you desired?

I share the view from train's window
with a school-uniform generation.
I don't quarrel. Enjoy too much teasy antics.
They're intrigued with trifles, so am I.
Someone's smuggled on board a blow-up piggy.
Between huffs of laughter, passes it round,
invites everyone to kiss its spongy snorter
with a peck or a smackeroo. The smart lad,
under guise of friendship, asks the wise lad
at just the right moment for the answer
to a classroom conundrum
then returns to his 'I'm not bothered' stance.
Some teenage girls click-open compacts,
brush back, make new faces
for cubbish males collecting for a peep
or argue like advocates.
Suddenly, in the just-applied shadow
beneath a pair of brown eyes, I see gathered
my life desires and indiscretions under sheets.

I hope she finds gentle sex when her world's knocked dead.

The terrain's blemishes form a continual going-away
as if unflinching, my love keeps looking
straight into my face, yet walks backwards
beyond blurred outline, into absence.
'Gone Missing'. Neither an urgent act
or a patient retreat in love or war.

Freakish: pull of attenuated cords
that fastens us to a place on earth,
entwines us to other human beings,
brief quiver can break, divide.
From where I sit,
through landscape of banishment
though not spectacular
I travel toward a brightening future
that reached, is as unlit as yours,
my dear brother.

With you in mind, down seventeen miles of track,
thoughts have breached acquired defences.
Outside, my straw fortresses pass.
As the journey narrows toward departure
on the left, an eccentric garden of flowerless mounds
where vestiges of Bishop Alexander's Castle
stand interred, each sign-posted for the visitor to plot
in shot-grey air, iridescent blues and reds.

Now the battle isn't won or lost
in vapour-looping dogfights,
an anxious British boy attending, binoculars focused,
his bicycle primed to capture fallen Germans.
Conflicts are enacted that re-echo as ours.
Spectres of cruel acts distort our future.
We've damned other country's present.
No making amends.
Give up on the re-entering dawn,
accept the long Tenebrae, out-endure the dark.
Nerves are inured to diurnal change.

All turn. Nocturnal apprehensions cease.
White flags and khaki turn to colourless fabric.
Hate, mistrust and aggression
(not as if the time-scale can be engineered,
shift from old to new,
a millennium standing as a strong divide)
one must give up on such whimsies.
Change strikes at the least documented hour.
Finally, passage of time washes out the irony.

Slowing by pasture, crosshatched fen, more than irony stays
in level fields of quill-thin stubble
and harrow-churned earth. I imagine
crewmen re-entering the safe air-zone,
undercarriage shot away, carrying back
riddled victims. For the survivors
what's there to do? Subdued welcome
with embracing smile, de-brief,
drink a mug of best brew
before projecting wings, once more blot the sun.
Novice sky-combatants –
nylon chutes daintily packed – came from remote regions
of a commonwealth to defend British wolds, fells and rivers,
once-a-day stations and cathedral cities,
as if their *terra matrix*.

I follow my namesake. June 1940:
his speckled tanned arms work the sickle
in an east coast hayfield. I follow in September
when wings sickle the air and he fights for life
as he spirals on fire down through cumulus.
You could hear them you know,
over the radio, you could hear the chat,
their screams... the horror...

Brother, when we misread the maps,
stumble head first into a field of the crowded dead,
we mustn't forget him with his winged collars gone
or a teenage woman's compassion for a stranger.

Where's the sense in such commitment?
There's a part of Lincolnshire that remains
forever Canadian (to extend Brooke's metaphor);
a patch of torn ground perpetually Polish,
a spot under shattered branch tops always Punjabi,
a privet-watching confine that's Caribbean.
When de-mobbed, displaced survivors came back,
and other émigrés inspired from imperial-tied cultures,
they were shunned.

Wanting to fold bravely creased trousers
over a bed-sitter chair, were offered no room.
For decades, in blue and black scrawling
on white walls of our nation's toilets,
they have seen themselves condemned.
I hear talk groaning from ethnic fear,
blaring distrust of difference
loud as air-raid sirens through an island psyche.
Still the pub quorum blaffers: *They didn't give them guns
at first you know; couldn't trust them, those Blackies.*
An empire of people sought a nourishing core
and found its centre heartless.

For the indigenous
who've been spat on as they *linked out* hand in hand
with black or chestnut-complexioned outsiders
who helped rescue this country
once nearly drowned, I record lesser offences.
Near me: a young black girl
wearing the public school image
is still shunned, needs to belittle herself
to find a friend and can't imagine why.
Awkwardly up from my seat, gathering belongings,
the vibrating metal carcass judders to a halt.
My co-travellers look resolutely the other way.

Stepping off, finding a foothold on the scrappy platform
among the dispersing crowd,
nodding to several *excuse me*s,
memory slips. I almost forget all the journey called to mind.
Think only I must pack and travel onwards
– come and visit you, before too long.
                                      Now I know
my home's not mine no matter how often I return.

II.

Summer at No. 8

New owners
restyled the garden,
put in flags and café tables,
severed wild ivy that once
strangled shade offerings of tall beech.
Now overhead each green napkin
freely sings,

from an open pot,
yellow with mocha-brown highlights,
faces of pansies
are exposed –
the same as my ex-wife's
blousy delicate touch,

between pendant fuchsia
and bleeding hearts
a discursive
hover-fly,

no piped muse,
at a half-open window
a wind-charmer,

a coffee please,
a cappuccino, espresso
he goes up the range,

I say filter,
I'm not a regular here,
I feel a cat
approaching
from the blind side –

the owner and her son chat,
dropping the subject, picking it up,
the smell of bread baking settles over me,
they're flexing
for the onslaught of lunch
then their voices turn down,
remembering they've a patron
within ear-shot,
on the way out
the door squeaks too loud.

Harbour Mouth: Whitby

for Milner Place & Chris Firth

High summer cliffs shine
with morning gilt. Mist falls
bringing the horizon in reach.

I stand at the utmost wall
not far from the red-eyed tower
that guides purr of returning trawlers.

Distantly, behind such a sea fret,
once assembled warships hid, ready
to launch an attack on the hill-beaked abbey;
cutting serpent heads slit through.

A moment, as if on lookout,
muscles stiffen to raise the alarm.

A northern diver glissades
with dragon-curved neck.
A swift, hooked plunge, it's gone.
Over aroused surface, ripples dilate
at the fog-horn's repeat.

I hear below
fishermen's patter
from under planks of the pier
at the breakwater's concrete foot, as they lean
to cast their whining lines.

Tide's retreating. Channel-grooves
drain the sea's fingerprints.
Up shore, a statuesque tribe of gulls;
above, another scavenger loops
to light on the emerging sand.
At night, gliding the port's grey,
they're white spectres, bigger
than scale, a sudden raiding party.

At the first unshuttered stall
I have a mug of bitter coffee
with blue-plastic-clad dockers.
From a shed, a fish-auctioneer's
voice swells and dips. On pallets
massive boxes are muscled out:
packed in layers of ice crystals –
jewelled scales, last night's catch.

About midnight, I was hunting for food,
found an undimmed chippie. Under neon
an old woman, with weary politeness, asked,
Open or wrapped? as if for the ultimate time.
Open please. *Just 80p,* she said, *for the chips
that'll do. The fish isn't up to much.*

A huge gull back-flaps on a guardrail,
opens its nestling's beak. In leathers
an aged seadog with buckled wellies
marches right up and flings in an arc.
His bird gobbles each airborne bun,
stretching and straightening its neck
as the northern diver – after re-surfacing.

Below, cobbles and drifters sprawl
in clusters, mud-stranded. Each
prow signed with an enigmatic name –
Sophie Louise, Royal Sun and *Bricies*.
Broad or thin hawse, few go off the radar unnamed.
I try to guess what's told beyond the last log,
storm-intoxicated, trawling vast night
to trap tiny silver hoards, wrestle
machine arms, tight-cabled nets;
though no fisherman, as if a lover,
has welcomed or sought to lure me there.

I chance on a friend, a fellow
landsman, clean-shaven, smartly
dressed and bound for work. He gazes off
towards shapes anchored in prolonged twilight:
*It's timeless this place, anonymous,
as if you could never leave an impression.*

His address cracks a code starting a dialogue
till with hand-shakes as an oath of tomorrow
we part, before I turn towards my reflection
and a softened outline of the world's end.

Infant Land

Somewhere out of range
giant-shoulder hills rest
crystalline in flames of snow,
dark-jade ocean unfurls a tonnage of foam,
naked sandbars cringe; elsewhere freezing fog
glazes two lit-up ships, one bound for port,
the other toward open water.

In an ash bordered field, through
sunny patches, around cut-down trunks
pallid bushes are on fire with green buds.
I follow close my young guide's
lead through hollows
and over broken mounds.
Just outside his walled city
a newness blooms. A future
rises from the past. Once buried
under wreckage and toxins
guarded saplings burst,
outcast earth breathes, befriended.

We soldier on, picking up debris
a burning wind throws against
his infant land.

Up From the Coastal Route

Hill-jagged fir stands
and dry stone walls
pattern our June mood.
From side ravines
venous conifer roots
fan under knolls,
nearly exposed:
earth worn to a pellicle.
Ahead, outlines merge. We feel
sucked into tightening folds.

Like a vagina, you say
later. I keep thinking it's all
sublime entrance: no way through,
intimate, at any moment we'll need
to reverse down the valley.

Suddenly we emerge
into tufted meadows
and skylark-fields.
A village opens its stone arms.
At Slaidburn, zigzagging
from slate-walled house
to house, grey rooftile to tile,
sun's bunting celebrates
a shieldless Britannia,

who, from a memorial bench,
looks faintly scornful
as she awaits a once-a-day
connection. Soon,
we're climbing again toward
Cross of Greet, Catlow Fell,
once breathless summits
disappeared under storm-bursts,
wind-screams and earth-shakings.
Half way up we pass
on the road's gravel edge,
in full stride, the back-packing
isolated trekker I used to be.

Shadow of Earth

1.

Whispy Thirlmere's sombre.
My Canadian friend and I
worry for sunlight. Then
snap; his daughter complains
No more pictures of mountains.

2.

Moon's bone china chin –
black storm cloud withdraws, again
a fist advancing.

3.

Sculpted lioness, a tomb guardian,
reclines with hollowed eye-cups
that once, bold with limpid glass,
mirrored the Aegean's solar blue.

4.

At the rope-barrier a visitor
sees the Readers' Room climb
to a gold and mauve dome
that addresses an assembly
of paper-bound dreams.

5.

By the beechwood path
our history from Battle
of Trafalgar to Dunkirk
up-to-now is chronicled
by devolving snowdrops.

6.

Have you been here before?
side glancing eyes inquire.
Her long hair red as redwoods
we walk between, at Nocton,
along a thread of road.

7.

Under instruction: one leafless
avenue shadowed by the next –
L plates almost whacked off –
can't help being diverted by
loveliness of almond blossom.

8.

After the interview
as a last arrival,
heart ready to break,
at the station
black butterfly flutters
across the rails.

9.

Half-drowned in Madras
lemon's slippery curve
intimates childhood
– the ocean-slick back
of Babar's rescuing whale.

10.

Thirty three years in the past
from a liner's cutting prow
I leaned into the future,
plunging through mid-Atlantic.

11.

As day unravels,
lifting from shallows
almost like oars
a heron's slow wings
spread across the river.

12.

In pantomime
a gull struts the jutting shore;
drab algae waves lap
an unearthed amphitheatre,
the lake's rocky tiers
rows of ruined seats.

13.

The newfangled expressway flashes by
through the old deep-wooded escarpment.
I kneel where *Grandma* and *Papa* wished
to sleep, polish their violet-fretted bronze.

14.

On Donny station,
waiting a loop train south,
cold and peace-giving
streams of sun lustre
through a lattice sky.

15.

Beyond afterglow,
the shortest night
hesitates to break
bands of heliotrope
linking a still willow
to a stiller fir tree.

16.

So gradual an eclipse:
as if gravity's passion
too painful a memory,
the love shadow of earth
stretches over the moon.

Two Gardeners

One placed on a plinth a stone heron
to watch over their koi carp;
around with unnatural constancy
a mother and daughter laboured:
tended rose, hosta beds, green path
ways and vulnerable pond-sides.
Shared each year's needs, toiled
and gazed across trowel or secateurs,
unspeaking, narrated their hidden lives.
The older desired descent into darkness
ready to force a command; the younger,
on the brink of disobedience, wished
to split open earth to allow in light.
Who knows which faded away first,
from beyond the ornate gate, observed
the garden's concealed imperfections?
But then, on a simple platter, at dusk,
two overlooked cups collected dew
as if a subtle rapport would continue.

Somersby

I prosper, circled with thy voice
                    Alfred Lord Tennyson

Following a ploughed-over Roman road
I find Somersby and walk close-round
its grassy church, half read inscriptions.
I know no one in young Tennyson's home.
A red kiosk stands by a shy girl's yard gate
and beside the field a tractor, its engine off,
from the cab a two-way radio chattering on.
I approach the old rectory: maybe invited in
to stroll through the poet's childhood rooms
and corridors, find a whiff from musky walls.
But my civil knocks pass unnoticed. The older
Tennyson, among dazzling imperial tributes,
read *In Memoriam* to his jet-shawled Queen.
The way into here, and the way out, follow
the cultivation's contours as if everything fits
in this hamlet, as if an empire could relax
in the cupped palm of his unexotic hills.

The Deserter

Above whirring wheels
I cling to my window outlook, wanting
to push into ultramontane regions
moulded from twisting ravines
far from the call to arms.

In the bucking double-decker
at the front in the upper saloon:
an old soldier,
eyes blotto and limpid,
snatches my attention
I was in the Black Watch...
He shouts above the roar.
Spit straight
straight in an officer's face;
not bearing his insult.
Zzip, zzip, off came the stripes,
zzip, zzip down on the ground.

My father, in his country's uniform,
tried to make his return journey.
A fortnight he and his civilian friend
reached The Railway Tavern
for a farewell drink, then hours
with humour and reckless story-telling;
each evening they'd shamble back
to his friend's incredulous wife,
before in the morning, first thing,
he set out lucid once more to return.

I'm stretched, this journey,
further and further:
what prevails beyond arrival,
in mountainous interiors
at the end of maverick valleys
where retreat and extreme hubris
are at home, when anticipation of return hits
its vanishing point?

My dad didn't leave the war,
his khaki sleeves trimmed with stripes.

I visualise them
fluttering round his black buffed boots
as stretched ochre wings.

The Waiting Room

Unused seats crowd
the lit-up waiting room
bolted against
a stranded traveller.

Along the platform
under notices
latticed benches repeat.

Is it a disembodied breath
rocking the hinged sign?

In the dark flat pit
the double rails
turn to rust.

A slender-bodied
signal light
stands fixated on green,
burns into the distance,
mocking my late journeys

when youth's loneliness
seemed exhilarating: whole
metropolises flickered by
without one waving hand's
encouragement or welcome.

Where was I going –
to a fragrant lover's bedroom
that night,
who afterwards
fastened her door hard
against imagining travellers?

Did I jemmy open the front lock?

Through the ill-lit house
sneaked, bent over with doubt,
ascending the stairs
tall with hope, nudging ajar
the easily swung-open door:

she gleamed, from the window,
in her small corner bed,
as if never aroused
by a human hand.

At Asycoughfee

I held the door ajar. You stepped into the light.
Behind, inside the Hall, your shadow hesitated.
In grievance, you sharply said *Thanks Thanks*
as your white stick queried the grooved threshold.

Outside, across from you, I pulled up a noisy chair.
Imagined my lips seeking, in blindness, to kiss yours
as yours so often had sought mine. *Peace Garden's
full of soldiery plaques. Isn't that odd? Don't you think?*

Yes, but maybe soldiers pray hardest for peace.
Behind a male voice blasted, *If that ball comes close,
I'll pop it. All right?* You heard youngsters escaping.
I watched shadows move across old flags.

A sun-burst tensed your arms. In the background
a fountain's tight lips hardly spoke as water tickled
the surface of an ornamental lake. From the wings
a thousand tatty roses scented the air between us.

Canada – America

The train swings out along
Lake Ontario's shore
over bridged bays and inlets,
past once busy harbours
long silted into marsh, past
Jordan and Dalhousie that seem
to re-emerge, a thousand white wings
across the still open water's grey.

Passing acres of small naked trees,
a veteran conductress reveals
she loves to travel this route in spring
when from both sides, blossoms
white and pink overtake the orchards.

Next stop Niagara Falls!

Honeymoon capital of the world
she might've once crooned.

Against a Canadian-facing window
a passenger, crunched under her fur-lapel coat,
glances around, like me travelling alone.
A red and blue pom-pom, as if a parting corsage,
fastened to the grip of her big, weathery case.

Crossing the Niagara has never been easier,
the primal river's reduced to a leapable gush.

The train slows, squealing to rest in the border-zone.

U. S. customs officers step on board,
decorated with badges sublime as the Falls,
and dark-handled guns.
Just the facts, ma'am,
requires a vintage Dragnet detective.
The U.S. recognises one citizenship only,
states the official from his navy windbreaker, disowning
each hyphened nationality.

Out the stationary window
rusted sumac tops
and purple of wild raspberry canes
sway madly similar
to those on the other side.
Pearl necklaces
like contraband
embellish the glass.

Yesterday, in a downtown gift-store,
I peered hard into each jewellery case.
Excuse me, a female stranger
held up two objects
for inspection, *You're a man,
which of these rings do you think
my husband would prefer?*

After an irritating delay –
tracks from custom's vehicles
having left decorative arcs –
the train starts to edge forward, wheels
screeching toward the next arrival call.

At breakfast, my mother mentioned her travels
during the thirties' to New York City:
an excited young girl peering out
the family car's rear side-window.
Slowing up at some lights, a youth leapt
from nowhere on to the running board.
Cars had running boards then, mum inserted.
The boy hollered, *Got somewhere to stay?*
No! the joint answer. He grinned widely,
clutched a door handle, fixed his feet to rubber tread,
hanging on in Keystone Cop style, directed
the family to a nice clean hotel off Times Square.
She spoke as if perplexed by that outcome.
Him receiving from her dad a five-star tip.

States-side, back then, Canadian plates were rare.
During prohibition, a New Yorker fooled,
Haven't you guys smuggled some drink?
What other reason to tour dry America?
In another adventure, I was told, the family
obediently followed an AAA map into Harlem
and after a crazy day ended up begging for sleep.
OK! the hotelier finally conceded,
I guess we can sneak a few whities in.

At last we stutter into Buffalo.
Between railway cars, brash rain splashes
turning to indeterminate snow.

As again the locomotive gains speed,
I enter a conversation with an American
who begins almost at once
to trace his Italian Irish roots.
*My grandfather was murdered
in 1917. Killed in a village one night
in the Virginia coalfields, him and three others.
No immigrant's grave. Barbed wire pulled tight
round a tree marked where he'd died.
Grandmother, still carrying my father,
was a witness. The truth never came out.
I came back, years on, and saw a bulge
where the trunk had grown over his straps of iron.*

Across the café car's arbourite table
my fellow traveller stares away
then asserts, *I'm licensed to carry a firearm.
I never draw out my gun as a threat,
only to kill.* Far ahead the train hoots
a protracted warning
moaning onwards, 'Look out, Look out'
as a night flying bird's impassioned call.

I watch those brisk customs guards
with their black, polished revolvers
and I want to snatch the brute from its holster,
point the snout in their faces – reverse
that power – claim my right to self-annihilation.

Nearly all passengers have changed.
I glimpse in the shivering glass, myself writing
as if somehow getting to the bottom of it.
Frail winter orchards stretch back
toward a beginning blacked-out.
Remember, I should phone home when I arrive.

Through space, a tunnel's opened
as if, in a precognitive way, to see the unseen,
one more long drawn out hoot's expelled
toward Rochester, followed by Syracuse, on to Albany.

Lights flashing by grow remote as stars, until
between them and me, I imagine a cosmos.
My mother's journeys down New York State,
in her father's car, were glossed by a quest
for discovery: that kept the Rockefeller Centre,
Street Arabs, Empire State and '39 World Fair
on a human scale; made her dreams approachable.

At home, without a conspicuous illness,
she declines bit by bit toward a lesser
and lesser here and now, from which
there's no return, just as gran once claimed.
One day in the car, of herself and dad, mum said,
We're shrinking... Repeated the phrase –
I felt their expanding absence.

Through moisture-leaden night the horn
sounds and resounds; keeps surfacing.
When my destination is reached the train's
clicketty clack and prolonged hooting goes on.
Over a relaxed dinner, as a new dialogue starts
I attempt once more to find an image for that
arresting call... its abstruse, repetitive sounding-out.

Last Words

At Wickenby, through
the watch tower's museum glass,
on the western horizon
Lincoln cathedral glitters,
to the east old flight-paths
expand tranquilly in blue.

I hear crewmen huddled
in long-winged, rattling bombers,
after 'a soft target', Berlin or Cologne.
They come back skittering,
howling to land.

The tower's curator points
to an exhibit of detritus.
A Lancaster's
flak-riddled remains.
Call number displayed.
Every crewmember killed.

Should I grieve for concealed victims,
crushed under steel and mortar?
Wear black?

I stare, selecting a view,
separate finials
from blue-murder scream
of stragglers.

Thinned squadrons sighted
on the returning horizon
a frail figure of glass and stone;
from its ridge, the cathedral stood,
defied other winged attackers.

Some things survive.
The bomb aimer misses
or a target's no longer red.
Another edifice endures.
Mourners enter and bend
to touch a statue's toes;
toothpick-thin, flowery stonework
ascends above dust clouds.

How did anything survive?
Half-overgrown runways
look more insubstantial
than Lincoln's medieval facade.
Nor can someone's conviction
my love will return be final. Another
– arms at peace, sky's battledress removed –
walks across the welcome field
toward a lesser reunion.

I make eye-contact with the tower's guardian,
acknowledge his *thank you*
after he's outlined the task of transcribing
from torn, jotted down records,
last words of skippers, navigators
and tail-end Charlies.

At Staithes

Night sea hums beyond the breakwater.
The summer sky's
a field of gulls that thins and thins.
Some with mews swing in and away from cliffs
where black-backs with folded wings look down.
Most scavengers have settled
like ornaments set on terracotta,
in turn, accepting dark's long call for silence.

Crowbar Nab stands off.
Its eroded ascent
a black shape unwavering
in low water smoothed to inertia.

Horns of bay cliffs close-in,
leaving a thin exit for fishing boats
at 3 am. Ivory-textured, in tiers,
houses cluster against the hillside.
An upper window glows.

Along a dwindling shore
around colonies of hooded sleepers,
the rock faces crumble in whispers.
Hour by hour masterful profiles age.

From the slipway a harbour light –
glimmers on disordered sands –
then sends a beam glancing off the inlet.
Clandestine, the sea moves landward
lifting moored boats until they float
above their image of wooden bow and hull –
doubling chances of a good catch.

Half the beach has slid. Into blackness
the quay stretches like a crooked arm.
To see out night, many gulls have squatted
on a vast roof of the disused Ranters' chapel.
Now heavy steps of fishermen reverberate
from cobbled passages, zigzag stone stairs.
Whitewashed houses tremble.

III.

No Grimms, Andersen or Beatrix Potter

I remember a four-year old
with Athena eyes
who didn't wish me to read
from a favourite book
at bedtime; at mid-day
demanded stories to emerge whole
from my thought-entangled head.

I'm still unclear, when with sweeps
she painted a field-leaping horse
without a rider, if I should've set
a fiction on its golden back?

When she recited, dead fish were dead
and she'd never eat a thing from the dark ocean,
should I've lured her with a sea narrative?

I let serpents stand for omens of goodness,
journeys into black as footpaths toward light.

To my adventures'
slithery morals and disabled plotlines,
she stared up from behind the divan
out from under the stairwell
urging another fantasy.

One day I departed, walking
straight down the perennial path
out the child-resistant gate, not to look back.
A few passing words seemed kindest.

Ten years eclipsed.
Again I stood in an entrance,
struck another home's door;
my suitcase anxious with gifts,
volumes of journeyed words.
In the sun-touched front room,
curtains splayed, I waited
till at the wheeze of jeans
and tea-shirt a girl entered
with flashing eyes:
who was this visitor
and where'd he come from?

Hide and Seek

The tabby, of the woman I love, is dying.
Some odd hours dreams embrace fantasies.
Tufts of marbly fur under her dark belly
sway with freedom belying death's earliness.
She knows, my goldy grey-haired lover says.
I already hear her paws dancing across the clouds,
she adds sleepily before admitting the dark.

'Our love will last, won't it?' I ask alarmed.
Death's the extending dream, from which we hide,
that absence of being here that outlasts all else.
Being is death-defying and difficult to keep,
nine lives, or one, vanishes before fixed
in stone or sacrifice, as a friendship or love
sets a limit, turns and disappears through the thicket.

The Pond

I try to understand dark fathoms
of your fear, as when a child of yours,
not your only child, slid from the womb
into unsounded water, failed to emerge into light
when your twins were born. You sang
their birth and wept that loss. Sorrow
deepest as you held and stroked that nameless one.
Each pore felt the nothing slip away.

Each pond's green rim holds the solemnity
of unbroken waiting. You distrust mermaids,
the quick-finned, opalescent women who rescue
fabled mariner or baby from a downward spiral.
You understand, above that ancient mouth,
the sun-darkened surface never trembles.

She Wore Grey

The sky's murderous fragments
appear to converge
toward an inscrutable heart.

As wind chases hard at my back,
I think of her, shaking on her prison dress,
the one who didn't care if she was caught.
Standing at her mirror,
with a tucked-in knife,
she stroked hips then breast,
smoothing her unbearable looks.

I first saw this view

as a child
portrayed it
impressionistically.
Thin black vertical lines
forked, at times vanished,
as lines on the palm of a hand,
to create a fractured network
that ascended, yet was discontinued,
crossing at intervals
pink, grey and blue scarves.
Mixed colours
as an artist might imagine
the shortest day or sky's narrowness,
with horizontal twilit veins
stretching over a winterscape.
The earth was left, mystifyingly
blank – an endless opening.

Red Hawthorn-Hedged

I.

Red hawthorn-hedged, railside:
tawdry blankets hang
from chestnut backs
of grazing horses.

Steel-coupled carriages pass;
my seated reflection not yet
stealing the afternoon view
as later in the year.
The horses hardly lift inquisitive heads
already knowing human pursuits:
the hush following departure, frenzy before arrival.
All too minor to distract
blazing-eyed creatures.
They, if imagining a journey,
leap the hedge of night
to reach their constellation:
carrier of heroes or children
lost in mother's arms
in a Blakean masterpiece
or as Banshee. Railside,
patient hooves stir-up myths of Pegasus.

II.

At a coupling's jerk, I remember:
I once nursed; tried to soothe those
whose death-journeys had begun.
I stood beside overwhelmed men
and women, in restricted rooms;
listened, with strange intensity
to stories and dreams they told
before the next alarm's bleeping.
They were tortured many times,
thrust out of life into night,
hurled back into day's glare
before thrown into darkness –
exiting, and forced to re-enter.

At each, the shrinking heart howled.

Emerald-brown horses,
tails still on this flyless afternoon,
leapers of the sky or saddled with adventure,
death's a parting green to further wonder.
If pumping limbs stumble at the last hedge,
no matter, the beast needs to be shot.
If they're ribs scattered after vultures
in total stillness. A tapered skull
the rest riddled, buried: through oval sockets
space winnows in and out; their remains
shine like polished ivory
bones, turn fibrous lungs, breathing
the amazement of being here.
Breathing in death gives them wings.
I think both the horror and the wonder,
in a moment, eyes open, through
my lidless window as the train pulls
forward, leaving departure a screeching memory.

III.

I've tried to conquer death,
pre-empt birth,
occupied in twin brinkmanship.
When did a human being
observe the body's wrinkly arrival
and purply departure as event,
its perfumed out-of-the-womb,
its reeking into night? Saw birth
and death as the full moon's
sunniest opening?
Whatever my preoccupation
I've criss-crossed that openness –
that uncertainty – with webbing
precepts... cutting into the void
with a thousand and one pointed anticipations.
Have we once taken a chance on the unknown?
Risk being born or dying as a toss of dice
in a dim alley relying on beginner's luck?

Sorrel horses graze –
in moth-holed blankets
the stitched border torn, discoloured –
but their gated-field stays open
for one gambading on hind legs not under cavalry spurs
but constellations' heat. We can't conquer or pre-empt,
only telescope a beginning, defer disappearance
to a further hilltop, birth to an earlier valley.
I long to escape the obsession
to begin and end.
What of the unconquerable
in-between-ness
of the everyday here and now?
The sleekest flanked gallopers
have never once wanted to be first.
Human will overriding theirs, forced the chase.
Never once desired to be a seat for fishermen
to wade through waves higher up shanks
though seductive moonglow
on Mediterranean; not once a carrier of the sacker of cities.
Pegasus never desired a straddling lord.

IV.

When did I first long for the here and now?
I stared for miles from the rear side window
of my father's car; saw the moon
for the first time as free,
a winged-horse in silver disguise,
motoring as fast as dad's Pontiac
far advanced in age. Comfortable
in that tasselled-textured backseat
I had no yearning to return home.
I filled up with all that I watched;
the rear glass's soft curve sharing
curved muscles of that night-galloper.
I begged the journey not to end.
Here I am, after decades of journeys,
gazing from a train's round-cornered glass
still hoping for non-arrival, the sacred
in-between-ness of here and now.

V.

Love and sex once were the same:
leaving me mysteriously free,
neither compassionate nor cruel,
yet seized in passion's in-between-ness.
When limbs entangled
in the act that couldn't be
innocence or experience –
and never enough to master
but just beyond being enthralled,
though not yet lost – the world slipped
and longings became vibrant
and whispered in my ears that yearning for no end
till the past was a haziest non-beginning.
Why did I suddenly try to command it?
Enough to know the split moment
in secret, in closet, in a cupboard
under stairwell or a quickie inside the hangar's
clanging door: a Canadian airman
who has her tenderly against the wall
and says: *please, not now, your pleasantries*
or the way in a sticky July room she slinked off the settee –
living room curtains closed to keep out the heat –
and swam across the carpet as if footless
to where I sat hunched and read *Orlando* –
my unwrinkled nape against the window ledge.
I only had time to lift my head over the book's
horizon, before her bright lips
devoured me like a whale; I was a boat
gone down her beautiful throat.

Why ask passion to be pure,
bridled with a change of name
rimmed with gaugeable time when
it's that chance taken with the unknown
that devours and leaves us free?
How many times have we tried to corral
our small death's climax with a platinum ring,
some chorus of bells or more perishable
ribbon-tied lacquered sticks; giving that moment
of amazement a beginning, a meaning
when no items of belonging and measurement
insure love will be with us at our journey's close?

VI.

I've seen how eros
doesn't need 'the beautiful',
though the world rarely forgives
a grotesque body that desires.
Each passer-by turns from
the ugliness of disordered skin,
in the long ward, on the street corner.
Those rejected have felt love in their pores –
not masturbating or longing from windowsill,
strappeddown-chair or sickbed –
their contorted out-stretched hand
and face have asked no pity.
That body nearly torn in two
has sought no re-union.
I had, and knew *it* best
when no marking or sign was needed
before the carriage with flowery hoops rattled from a
    stable yard,
before the whip-slashed rump crossed the finishing line
and so, long after the jockey dismounted with a friendly
gee-gee and pat as his racer was led to grass,
steam rose from the currycombed flanks
and still tense fore-muscles,
molten ore in eyes; steam rose
from the dangling chestnut mane
of creatures that inhale the infinite,
whose bones chime with the unbeginnable
of space and time, who, at a certain hour,
we might rein-in through love.

VII.

Some affections still elude
imagining. Think of the sun-child's fate,
that returning mythos.
The father knows his son will ask
out of love; from love the father will yield
to his request. In deepest empathy
taking on that guardian guise
the sun's child chariot-rider
will crash out of existence.
The train speeds on

limps on. Each day I've stood
by disabled humans,
wrecked in chaotic flesh,
and seen how liberty horses bow
their gold-feather-heads
to a waxy or claw-like caress. I've heard
such humans utter but one phrase – and watched
them walk a mile and see it stretch to a hundred –
how their one or two coupled words become a poem's
sonorous colour, my crimson
tiger, my purple
jockey; an epic,
each round note from
shapeless mouths drooling speech
dripping from resinous lips
like pink chewing gum.

And if they have to stumble forward,
their eyes mis-located, staring from too high in the forehead
if missteps are a tripwire to fling them into an abyss,
there's no abyss. If their brain has pushed their skull
till it looks like a stone overhang,
it's only an image.
If they can't escape their
flesh's convolutions in roly bands of blubber
till the night nurse shuns
the sight and stink, slams the door;
if in a lukewarm room
they scream *it's cold*
then their home is elsewhere
but they are here on earth in view
naked to be loved or hated
just the same... like all of us
hardly here at all.

The glare
they use to pin
the able-bodied – rages:
do you think I'm rooted,
made to be ugly and dismissed. Look
– out of sight my excellence sings.

They are not oaks, lightning-split
and juddered down to ground,
a jagged god's bolt tumbling the sun's lover
from his father's auric car, the sun-father's boy
who merely wanted to guide the unsteerable,
ride flame-spinning wheels,

handle with hardly adolescent fingers
nocturnal horses
that ascend dawn and descend below dusk.
But those now and here disfigured, unwanted,
when you're lucky enough to have them approach
and their palm, like the pink concave of a splintered seashell,
is thrust in your face; it's not always for help.
Those whose awkward voices
pronounce a sentence or two –
crimson tiger purrs in middle of night,
purple jockey climbs a tree to stars –
they leave a sound
that can't be echoed to silence.
These, I've loved
though their bodies look
destroyed, hearts distorted.
And they are not more special
than the girl-child that her father
suffocated on his back seat
than another
that neighbours,
out on the street, kicked,
pummelled to death
his wasted limbs, stubby dissipated hands,
his already smashed-in face
with gormless blank-staring eyes.
I say: no murderer touched them.

At each blow the shrinking heart howled.

VIII.

These are thoughts along the way.
Cold. Hot. Dis-armed, un-faced, legs-cut-off,
a mouth incarcerated in stone, stone lungs that
breathe in bone-landscape of dead horses
that go on when inhalation's gone.
When will they break
from the earth's illusion,
take flight – transforming
landscape to wind, granite outcrop to air,
a night's caress under black poplars,
a gale, a tempest, a breeze?
Not enough to link images
incident to incident
or, sitting in a claustrophobic room,
hold a narrative between four walls;
each idea must dove-tail,
intermingle
with a further notion,
the next near-sighting of the infinite.

IX.

Look through an arch –
gargoyles above, garlanded with grieving figures:
the loss of mother, or child, a vacant cradle –
and stare into a blue-black
unclosable space. Stand on its lip like Pilgrim,
like Tosca, breathe in the next step.
I only imagine
to walk across a floorless expanse.
Climb long stairs to a threshold:
stone steps warped by use,
so unsafe that holes for new
newels and railings have been drilled
but not yet fitted. As the ascent
increased, confidence grew
that many had scaled...
spiral stairs to nowhere.
Now turn back
to discover the foundation's spun away,
a disordered spinning top.
There's nothing for it but settle on the bottom step,
take off shoes... and let feet touch the abyss
as once I sat on flagstone brink
of a pond made to infinity's shape,
let my thin bronze legs paddle,
untroubled by gold-red slivers
sensuously coiling
in and out between. Lodged
in the interim of the here and now,
unafraid of falling, I sense a part –
often discarded, just stumbled on

absent-heartedly, with no name to call it –
my winged persona. Certainly not a whole,
perhaps a fragment,
a bit of a stained glass,
broken glint on the ground, that other self:
nothing to be proud of, or something anyone
would wish to be wedded to, hire at Michaelmas
or award in a stadium. The brittle shard
an earlier age named soul,
envisaged, formed
from a deified mind.
Still undefeated
it's formless figure
that might be chanced on in a dream,
no rock to build faith
as if a bronze coin housed in a tree's cleft
to which someone returns
era to era and finds its dull
metal circle still there; instead, it's like a glimmer of glass
that you don't know is an obstacle till your fingers bleed,
a bit of light chased over a field,
a will o' the wisp of substance; something lost,
rediscovered, misplaced
then found again, then hidden
brilliant but unseeable,
seen as nothing,
mistaken until at death's brink
we long to catch that metallic shine,
to cut, polish, to make a key to open,
with a timid shoulder-shove, the unknown.

X.

Circus horses lower their heads to nibble,
their billowing feathers out of view
not to disturb nagsman or trick-rider.
What would they think
if they saw wings unfurl like sails on flying ships
ready to leave the paddock's harbour?
I imagine a part of me like Pegasus
wings out-spread: bones breathe,
the universe plays
the instrument of thinning ribs,
air in gusts singing
between bowed bars.
I will have taken off this body
like a piece of clothing
gently disarranged on a bedroom chair
awaiting morning. Someone may
wear it better, trim it more tastefully.
I'll be elsewhere – out of flesh.
This desire plucks
my heart: to be free from the need to arrive
to outrace time and released
from the call to return, as if we could slip back
through a key-hole to an initial departure,
rewrite the plot. Return can't rescue the present
but leaves the knight errant
exhausted, entangled. Retrieval
lies in no yesterday or tomorrow
only in the briefest splice.

That discarded instance has come and gone –
we've all owned it.
A moment took us by the hand; we accepted a few courteous
curvetting steps, but prickling grew in nervous palms –
as it does sometime when dancing with a loved one,
as a child holding a grandfather's monumental grasp
or a dying father's – suddenly our grip
falters and we have to let go,
our ears ready to burst
from listening to the never-ending.
Elegant creatures nub blades,
no longer summer-bright,
not yet matted with frost or lost below a bank-breaking river,
still the sun tingles enough to make roan coats shine
in that present *they* occupy
like the most inconspicuous tenants
waiting for us.

XI.

Longings will pass.
This journey slow to completeness long long before
unboarding, the platform prepared with a shout and silence
to greet the in-comer. Can't remember when I left.
My setting out's disappeared, fold over fold like endless
   clothing,
myth inside myth. It's only a guess when born;
how many shapes wrapped in.

XII.

One day Justine told his companions
half-way up a wooded slope –
mules plodding a lower field's verge –
that he was ready to leave the earth.
Saw his body no more than
a thing a child consumes then flings out.
Seeing his friends' downcast expressions
he attempted to console.
Brightening, one asked,
Where are you going from here?
'There are many journeys'.
Another came back,
thinking of the now aged man's
once strong will,
Which have you chosen?
'They're all beyond grasping.'
Then, demanding none pursue, Justine turned
and disappeared into the thickening wood
a time of year when snow's young.
A crimson cardinal flimmered,
mild browns of a female, lighting near,
filled the bare undergrowth with delicious song. Then
day went mute but for the fading squeak of his feet.
Some years later
at the imagined site his past companions
planted a small monument
with his words imprinted. You can find it still
if you chance on the path,
no signpost marks the way.

As I came, seeking, I saw a young girl
leading down the track a huge white horse,
behind her its curvaceous form floated.
Its streamlined head damask
around the nose; high its eyes
looked forward, swollen
with afternoon light. Its legs tapered
and vigorous, ready to gallop, but I noticed
the calm each hoof angled from the turf
in turn was set a foot or so ahead.
The master led by the novice.
Her tiny hands guided its pulsing body.
I thought only love must have in-rein that will.
You could come to the stone marker,
examine bronze lettering impressed,
syncopation of phrase,
words' disablement,
one letter not the same as the next:
the gripped chisel that made hollows
to hug each shape, that mis-struck;
notice, varying distance between each.
You could breathe in
a stone fragrance that weathering exudes
though someone scrapes moss away from time to time
then rubs till – *Justine said: I'm ready to leave the earth* –
shines almost new. Not quite an oblong rock
in a heap that walkers leave,
but the marker
has transmogrified almost into the terrain –
it's easily missed – its ensiform peak long blunted.

You could stoop and touch a knubbly surface,
feel igneous gradations with flecks of quartz and mica;
homing-in see more nicks, gouges
the maker couldn't touch-up, the second thoughts; see
style's asymmetry; bruised margins of bronze; but strain
    closer,
on eye level with the words, staring into the formed stone's
micro-pebbly surface, its tinted variations,
and it might turn transparent
to be an open window
through which you can see
on a further hill-line resting
your wings of Pegasus folded
ready for you... as interim earth ends
and the unknown of existence begins.